TOOLS
for
FULFILLMENT

TOOLS

for

FULFILLMENT

HOW TO RECOGNIZE YOUR TALENTS
&
EXECUTE YOUR KNOWLEDGE

GREG DOBSON

Canadian Cataloguing in Publication Data

Dobson, Greg, 1964-
  Tools for fulfillment : how to recognize your talents &
execute your knowledge.

ISBN 0-9687965-0-8

1. Self-actualization (Psychology) 2. Young adults—Life
skills guides. 3. Self-management (Psychology) 4. Success—
Psychological aspects. I. Title.

BF637.S4D62 2001   158.1'084'2   C00-901408-X

Illustrations by Ellyn Sennema
Text design by Susan Thomas/Digital Zone
Cover by Intuitive Design

Printed in Canada by Queenstone Printing, Mississauga, Ontario

E.Y.E Publishing

CONTENTS OF THE TOOL BOX

**PLEASE GO TO THE
LAST PAGE**
(page 101)

ADDITIONAL TOOLS

www.energizeyourenterprise.com

Click on resource page

AUTHOR'S NOTE

The people in our world who have attained their visions and desires, who have created fulfillment in their lives, have a common thread. It is what I call CTC — Courage, Trust and Choices. The *Courage* to be involved in and experience activities; the *Trust* in their talents and abilities; the ability to make the right *Choices* that gave them the opportunity to be involved in their desired activities.

The question is, how do you cultivate *courage* and *trust*? My belief is that courage and trust are cultivated through experience and a personal philosophy that sets you free of preconceived ideas and notions. They are also cultivated by taking the time to recognize your talents and learning how to execute your knowledge to make *choices* that will take you down the road to exhilarating accomplishments and achievement.

The "Tools" presented throughout the book have been designed to help you create that CTC. Like a toolbox, the book is broken down into compartments, and each compartment contains sets of tools to help you. In Compartment 3, you will find exercises that will help you align yourself in the direction you want to go. The exercises were put together in one compartment instead of scattering them throughout the book to make the book easier to use.

My intention was to make the book as short as possible, leaving out the fluff, so you can get through it relatively quickly and use what works for you.

Each one of us has the ability to be fulfilled and achieve our visions that will enhance our life and those around us. The more tools and experience we have in relation to those visions, the closer we get to them.

As I once heard a fellow CAPS (Canadian Association of Professional Speakers) member, Tom Stoyan, Canada Sales Coach, say, "Your life can either be lived by design or by default."

Now that you have a set of tools in your hand, follow the example of the many fulfilled achievers and make the choice to live by design.

Enjoy the ride,

Greg Dobson

ACKNOWLEDGEMENTS

Mom, Dad and Scott, the real cultivators. ☺

Queenstone Printing Services (Gail, Terry, Tisha, Cary, Troy and Todd) for printing this book, but more importantly, for their ongoing support over many years.

All the people who originally proofread the book and encouraged me to continue: Annabella, Maryanne G., Peter, Jennifer, Cathy, Lina, Valerie, Q-ball, Rychard, Maggie, and Lois.

Mrs. Christie, some things just take time.

Every young and old person who shared their stories with me.

Heather Sproule and the late Dr. Paul Steinhauer for being wonderful mentors.

Elizabeth Verwey, for keeping me balanced.

Barry & Anne Colbran, for the countless hours you put aside to listen and give me some perspective.

Sam & Irene Bitensky, for exposing me to many different opportunities.

ALIGN THE MIND

What is it that you truly want out of YOUR life?

If today was the last day of your life, would you have accomplished all that you wanted to? Would you be disappointed if you had not accomplished some of the things you could have?

I'll let you in on a little research. Many people, when they get to 60 or 70 years old, feel disappointment. They wish they had done fulfilling activities that could have been easily accomplished if they only had the right tools and a little courage. Forty years from now, do you want to feel dissatisfied with your life? I think not!

To achieve, produce, build, create *anything*, we need tools. Tools are an important part of our daily life. Having the right set of tools can be the difference between enjoying the process or being frustrated by it.

As mentioned on *The Last Page* of this book (you did go to the last page first. didn't you?) "Tools" can be anything from ideas to philosophies to the tangible. The most important tool we possess, however, is *our* potential, our own unique

1

talents. Unfortunately, most of us do not recognize our innate talents or do not know how to use them for our own benefit and the benefit of others.

To understand *what it is* we are good at, we must do two things. First, we must consciously be aware of our skills and unique abilities and not take them for granted. The second thing we must do is gain experience. Experience expands knowledge. Increased knowledge enhances experience, leading to a more fulfilled life. Just think of the few experiences you have already had in your life. What would your life be without them, and how did they move you to have more experiences? The first time you drove a car. The first time you went on a trip outside of your neighborhood. The first time you kissed someone. Unless you have experience, you will never know. There are more experiences than any of us will ever get the chance to try. Don't let that limit you!

After reading about the lives of great achievers, I found their success comes down to the same thing — "Match your talents to a worthwhile purpose and never stop pursuing a better way of doing it. There is no path to achievement with fulfillment without the willingness to spend countless hours of trial and error." And if you like what you are doing, it won't matter how much time you spend at it!

We must "align our mind" so that we go after the experiences that best suit *our* talents and desires, not someone else's idea of what we *should* be doing. A little CTC will put us in the right direction.

COURAGE, TRUST AND CHOICES

CTC. No, not KFC — hang in there. CTC — Courage, Trust and Choices. With these three tools we can take control of our lives and believe me, if we do not, somebody else will.

We must have the courage to experience life and to achieve beyond our wildest dreams.

We must trust in our abilities and be willing to be patient over the long run.

We must make choices that will guide us into the direction of our desires, instead of choices that make us ask later, "Why did I make such a poor decision?"

CTC is vital to achieving fulfillment.

Courage. You will be tested to keep yourself focused on the direction of your desire. Think of a competitive downhill skier. This person needs to be 100 percent in control of their actions, their vision and their direction, and have the courage to be tested on a downhill run where one mistake could take them out of competition or result in serious injury or even death. They must make sure their equipment is in great working order and that they themselves are in top physical condition. A competitive skier races to the best of their athletic ability. They have no control over the other skiers in the race and can only focus on their own abilities and talent. If we put the same courage, focus and control into our lives, fulfillment and achievement will be realized.

Now, there are some of us who don't have the courage to even start in a direction we would like to go, never mind staying focused on it. Within the covers of this book are the tools to help you cultivate that courage. Cultivate — you know, like gardening or farming. How big, how strong, how far that little seed reaches to the sky all depends on how well it is cultivated. You too can be strong and reach to the sky and touch your dreams!

Trust. To continue briefly with the previous example, if the skier does not have trust in their abilities, they will never reach their full potential. It is sometimes hard to have trust when we lose our direction, or don't even have a direction in the first place. The exercises in Compartment 3 will restore or give you the trust that you need to get on with your journey.

We live in a time when we expect results immediately, and the word "patience" is slowly fading from the dictionary. We sometimes rush from one thing to the other trying to accomplish as much as we can, and we never seem to get where we want to go. If you have trust in your abilities and your plan (see Exercise 10), how quickly you get your destination becomes irrelevant. It is the exhilaration of the journey. (The skier gets 100 percent of their rush from the race, not stopping at the end looking at the clock.)

Choices. We all make choices. What we decide to do now, ultimately is where we will be in the future. We have to make the choice to seek out and understand our real talents and desires, and to make the further choice as to how to pursue those desires. Life is all about choices. There are no excuses — only the limitations you put on yourself.

An example of a good choice would be to associate with people who have desires like yours. Mike "Pinball" Clemons and most of the other inspirational figures of the 20th century have said that you must associate with people who share the same desires or have knowledge in the areas of interest to you.

Today, there are many associations that relate to almost every activity you can think of. Look in your library or on the World Wide Web under associations to find listings.

Become a member of those associations that match the activities that you find interesting. Give what you can to those activities and take the time to learn the processes that will help you accomplish your desires. Talk to experienced individuals who have overcome obstacles on their journey, so that you can find ways to avoid those obstacles and enjoy your journey more. Many of these individuals have spoken the phrase, "I wish I knew then what I know now." Put their experience to use to enhance yours.

Many parents who have achieved a great deal have encouraged their kids to follow in their footsteps. Not all of us have family members who can guide us, and this is why we must seek out people with whom we can build a mutually beneficial relationship. There is a variety of mentor programs available, and many of the mentors say they get as much out of the experience as they give.

The idea that every person must experience trial and pain to learn is ridiculous. People will help others learn by telling them about pitfalls that can be avoided. Make the choice to learn and to associate with people who can cultivate the will in you to go after your desires. Don't miss out on fulfillment and catch yourself later in life saying, "If I only knew then . . ."

───────────────

A great example of the use of CTC comes from a young woman who never gave up on her desire to be what she wanted to be.

Allena wanted to become a firefighter from a very young age. At the age of ten, she had an opportunity to talk with a number of firefighters who had responded to a call in her neighborhood. She was very impressed with the fire crew and decided then she wanted to be a professional firefighter.

As early as high school, Allena started making *choices* that would direct her toward her desire to be involved with community service. When Allena entered high school, she volunteered for a number of groups that had connections with the fire department.

After she completed high school, Allena prepared to take

the tests necessary to be a firefighter. Unfortunately, she found out that she would not be able to pass the eye exam.

Allena then took control of her desire and had the *trust* that one day she would be a firefighter. She decided that if she could not become a full-fledged firefighter at this time, she would do the next best thing. Allena joined the volunteer firefighters in her community.

During this time, Allena began working as a sales representative with a large organization. After ten years the company started laying off people, and in her late twenties Allena found herself suddenly unemployed.

During this ten-year period Allena kept close ties with the volunteer fire department. And she was able to take advantage of a new technology for restoring people's vision – laser eye surgery. Allena used her severance package and a bank loan to have laser surgery on her eyes. She had the *courage* to undergo the operation, and with her new 20/20 vision, she was now able to apply to the fire department. Allena's *trust* finally paid off. With advancements in science, technology and shared knowledge, never give up; we have no idea what is around the next corner.

Allena's application was accepted and she wrote the admissions test. The next stage at that time was the physical endurance test, which required applicants to run around the perimeter of a gymnasium five times. At the end of each lap, the applicant had to run through tight spaces between stacks of tires. On the third lap, the applicant had to climb over a six-foot fence and, at the end of the last lap, drag a dummy body weighing 180 pounds for 50 feet. The applicant had to complete the course within two minutes and nine seconds!

The first time Allena tried, she didn't finish the course. She was never a great runner and the air in the gym was very dry. Applicants were given two tries, and she did complete the course but needed two minutes and 20 seconds to do it. That meant Allena had to wait for a whole year to re-take the test!

Allena trained really hard and took the test again the next year. Her time fell short by 11 seconds on the first try, and by only six seconds on the second! Six months later, Allena was allowed to try again. Allena's time was good and she knew she was going to pass, but at the very end of the course, when she was dragging the 180-pound dummy, its arm got caught on a pole and the body fell on her and she couldn't get up. It was really frustrating because Allena knew she had the course licked. At that moment, Allena really wanted to give up and never wanted to take the test again.

Then there was a change in the hiring procedure, which introduced a different physical test. Although it had been about two and half years since Allena had first applied, and some of her friends thought she was crazy to keep trying and always failing, Allena was focused and committed because she wanted this so badly.

Allena started to train for the new physical test. She hired a personal trainer and took courses offered at the college and university — anything that would help. Allena ran all the time, even though running was still a hard thing to do. And she built her own endurance course to improve her chances.

The new test required applicants to run around a large area six times, while changing directions on command. On each lap, they had to climb a set of stairs four times, perform two knee-high jumps, do a vault and fall either on their front or back and immediately get up. Near the end of the test the applicants had to use a weight machine to lift 80 pounds off the floor, hold the weight and move it in six large arcs. After five attempts to beat the time on this new test, Allena finally passed by three seconds!

Within her first year with the fire department, Allena had

experiences like the ones those firefighters shared with her almost 20 years before. Allena accomplished her desire because she *cultivated* her *courage* by continuously being involved in activities associated with her desire. This in turn helped her make *choices* that supported her journey.

We all have the chance to achieve our desires, but we must be willing to be consistent and committed to the *process* that will enable us to achieve. We will get into the process in more detail later in the book, but we must make sure our *mind is aligned* and not justify why we *can't* achieve what we *want* to achieve.

JUSTIFY, JUSTIFY, JUSTIFY

THE HUMAN EXPERIENCE

"Ah, one more missed test, what's the big deal. . . . It's okay, I'll do the one next Tuesday, June 2, because I hear it's a good month and the right day to do a test because it's a new moon. Besides, I'm only 19 and grade 11 will still be here next year. Last night was a night I couldn't miss, chatting on the Internet to someone who lives in Japan — cool — and . . .

Here is a dictionary definition for excuses: 1. To overlook or pardon because of *circumstances* or some other reason. 2. To *justify* a fault or error.

Are we good at making excuses or what? No kidding. "It's too hard. It's too far. I *can* never do it, anyway. I have a family now so I can't take risks. I had a bad childhood. My big toe makes it hard for me to walk."

BIZZZZARRE. We can become professional "justifiers" or excuse–makers, with some of us already vying as qualified contenders. The variety of excuses is as vast as we are different.

Think for just a minute. Look at where you are right now. Look around and see all the different things close to you. How do you think you were able to get where you are right now? We can fly around the world and launch rockets into deep space because the Wright brothers continued to experiment even though they had lots of reasons to justify why they should stop trying.

Thomas Edison conducted 10,000 experiments before he knew success. Most of us would have quit after ten, never mind ten thousand. Henry Ford had very little education but his invention of the assembly line changed the course of industrial history. A whole book could be devoted to stories about various individuals who decided not to justify why they should stop, but forged ahead against the odds.

But some people will still say, "Oh yeah? But they had different *circumstances* than me, you know. I'll bet they had it easier than I do." JUSTIFY, JUSTIFY, JUSTIFY.

Here is what the great Bernard Shaw had to say on circumstances: "People are always blaming their circumstances for what they are. I don't believe in circumstances. The people who get on in this world are the people who get up and look for the circumstances they want and if they can't find them, make them."

PERSPECTIVE

Putting your life into perspective (see Exercise 7) can make those frustrating, debilitating, angry days seem relatively benign. We all have days that are, let's say, trying. But some of your *trying* days might be *easy* days to others. It's all a matter of perspective.

Now you may say, "Perspective is irrelevant; my day was a disaster and it feels very painful to me." There is no denying that, if it feels painful to you, then it's painful! But what you can do is to create a journal called "Perspective" that includes stories of people who have endured painful events, to help you deal with and give perspective to *your* painful events.

Here are a few short stories about people you may or may not know to help get your "Perspective" diary started.

Sandra Schmirler was a person who radiated love and compassion. She took up the sport of curling in her small hometown in Saskatchewan and within a relatively short time won a Gold Medal at the Winter Olympics. But her real dream was to have a family, which didn't seem possible for her to do. Then, she had two children she adored.

A few months after the birth of her second child, Sandra was told she had cancer. Within a year, at the age of 36, Sandra passed away.

Another young woman went in for a routine operation. When the doctors were operating on her they accidentally sliced her bowel without knowing. A few days later she was rushed back to hospital as toxins had leaked into her body. Unfortunately, too much time had passed and the doctors needed to amputate her hands, and also her legs below the knee, to save her life.

It is a good idea to put stories in your journal about people who have accomplished unbelievable feats. One that I have heard of lately is about a blind gentleman from Alberta, Mr. Watson, who is attempting to climb the highest mountain in Canada. Amazing.

It is very important to keep your life in perspective and

enjoy the day that lies ahead, because you never know what might happen tomorrow.

If you want a more lasting and visual perspective, go to the nearest hospital for sick children in your area. Usually within five minutes, you'll feel pretty lucky about the life you have, and if you're not using your full potential, you may also feel a little guilty.

Unfortunately, some of us need to be pushed into making our life the way we have always really wanted it to be. When a real tragedy hits close to home, we see how fragile our life really is and how our luxuries become less important. I never have been able to understand people who complain about never having enough money, or that they're not living a life of luxury, or the bad day they've had, just as they hit the power button for one of three TVs they own while warming up in their 1,500-square-foot apartment after coming home from a weekend of skiing in the mountains! Okay! Okay! *You* don't have it quite that good — you only have *two* TVs.

"Luxuries" are just that. We don't *need* them, but it appears our wants are becoming needs, and our needs are taken for granted, creating an unbalanced perspective.

When your life seems unbearable, take out your "Perspective Journal" and see how good your life really is.

Keep *everything* in perspective; it keeps you grounded. It makes you appreciate what you have. It makes you strive to reach your real potential.

THE S&F VIRUS

There is a terrible virus that has been spreading throughout North America for some time. Most of us have caught it and still have it. If not, beware — it is trying to attach itself to you as we speak. It is called the S&F virus — the Success and Failure virus.

We tend to qualify our lives based on whether we are successful or not. The only time we can judge whether we've been successful or not is at the end of something. But the end of what? At the end of a project or commitment? I don't think so. Because the end of a project or commitment always leads to another project, and you always take something with you from the project you have just completed. A job, an activity, a relationship, anything we do, regardless of whether we have deemed it "successful" or not, really carries on. So in reality, everything is just a continuation, and the only time we can really be judged as to whether we have been successful or not is at the absolute end — of ourselves. And will we really care at that point?

I often hear "Well what is wrong with being successful or trying to succeed at different things?" What really makes a person successful is always up to interpretation. When is a person a failure? We only know this at the end, and we have covered that. The problem with the mindset of success and failure, especially today, is that we are so focused on being successful. You could literally teeter-totter back and forth from success to failure on a daily basis. Say you ace a test today, but tomorrow you fail big time. Does this mean you're a failure?

When a baseball player wins the batting crown in professional baseball, his average is usually in the high .300s or low .400s. This means he didn't make it on base more than half the time he went up to bat!

Thomas Edison undertook 10,000 experiments before he invented the light bulb. Does this mean he failed 9,999 more times than he succeeded?

What these examples show is that people who achieve great things don't look at success or failure. They say to themselves,

"What can I do today to improve over yesterday and make tomorrow better." If you were Edison and judged yourself every day or month or year as to whether you were successful or not, and decided to continue or stop on that basis, we'd still be in the dark!

The point is, why be concerned about success or failure when you can concentrate on doing what you know is productive and enjoyable and will enhance your life and the ones that surround you? Each and every day is full of intrigue and excitement. If in today's world you are not intrigued every day and you suffer from boredom, well, you're already dead. Success or failure is in the eye of the beholder, and the only "I" that matters is yours!

If you're excited about the day that lies ahead, you *will* enhance your life and the ones that surround you, and success or failure will become irrelevant words and really have no meaning, except for those still trapped within this illusion.

The people who achieve fulfillment are the ones who stay unattached to outcomes, which allows them to improve themselves and improve the lives that surround them.

If you still feel the need to use the terms "success" and "failure," attach them to the journey. As long as you are on a journey to your desires, then you are "successful."

THE GOLF GAME

Earle Nightingale shares a story called "Acres of Diamonds" in his program *Lead the Field*. The story is about a rancher who sold his ranch and went from property to property looking for his fortune, only to find out that diamonds were discovered in a stream on his original ranch. The point of the story was we should work our own land before looking elsewhere.

This is very good point, especially true for today. We live in times when things are changing rapidly and it can be hard to decide what path to follow. This book will hopefully give you the tools to help you make that decision, but it's also very important to think about the pace we take.

I was talking to a friend of mine the other day, and she was telling me that she was frustrated because she wanted to get into the music industry, and she felt she was not being productive enough, or getting there fast enough. She used an example of other people who were doing part-time jobs and working their way into the music business. She felt she was lacking something because she was not getting ahead. The problem was that she was comparing herself to others. It is a big mistake to make to compare our achievements to anyone else's.

Maybe they have put more time towards their goal than we have.

Maybe they know someone in the industry and have gotten a break.

Maybe they don't have the S&F virus and you do!

We tend to look at other people and think, "Boy, they have got it together," when in fact they feel the same frustration and anxiety that we do. They just don't show it on the outside.

How many times have you looked across a room at someone who is well dressed and confident, and think to yourself this person has achieved a lot, only to speak with them and find out they have similar fears as you?

We must do ourselves a huge favor and not compete with others — only compete with yourself.

Just as in the game of golf, we try to beat our best score, and not the people we are playing with, because we're all at different levels. This parallels our life experience. We all have unique learning and life experiences that happen at different times than other people. It is impossible to compare yourself with anyone, and I mean anyone! We as individuals are always at different levels. Think about this because it is very important. It gives you breathing room, takes away your anxiety, and allows you to go at your own pace. Don't ya feel better already?

But it is important, when you are going at your own pace, that you don't start justifying where it is you want to go. There are a lot of people on the road to no-where-ville with two flat tires and no tools.

GETTING OUT OF THE CURRENT

What is the reason most people *do not* go after what they believe in, or *do not* act according to what really inspires them, even if they understand the principles of CTC?

Perhaps the answer is that people *never really take the time* to find out what their unique talents are. People hold themselves hostage because of things they've done in the past. And then there are people who continue to justify why they *can't* or *won't* do anything.

Others just fall into the river and go with the flow. I call this "The Niagara Syndrome" or societal current. We get caught in this current of patterns in our society and never swim free. But we *have* the ability to make choices and control where it is we want to go with the time and energy we have, but many of us choose not to.

My final "align the mind" philosophy may not be one all of you will subscribe to. But even if you don't, it will force you to look at why you make some of the choices you do — or are about to.

Most people live in a "societal current." They are brought to the river by previous generations and told to *go with the flow*. The problem with going with the flow is that your own unique talents will forever be underwater, and eventually the river will take you over the falls!

First of all, we are individuals possessing different abilities and visions, that are different from other members of our family. At a young age, if we have an idea that does not fit the norm, we are told to forget about it, and are sometimes even ridiculed. Our uniqueness, then, never becomes a factor in our life.

I remember the comedian George Carlin's line, "Why doesn't anyone make their own path? There's Bill over there, walking through a field with lots of open space and we say, 'Hey, Bill, over here on the path.' Like this is the only way to get to where you want to go."

What exactly am I talking about? Let me explain.

There has always been this notion that if you worked hard to get a good education, your life would be fulfilled. How many people do you know who have satisfying jobs that relate directly to their formal education?

Not many.

How many people do you know, and this may apply to yourself, who have worked hard at something, and have yet to find that fulfillment? How many people do you know who get really excited about their day? How many wish they were doing something else as a career?

Depending on your culture, at approximately the age of 22 we finish getting our "good education" (50 years ago it was age 15). We get engaged to be married between the ages of 22 and 25 (50 years ago it was age 16 to 19). We marry by the age of 27 (50 years ago you would be celebrating your 10th anniversary). You and your spouse rent or buy a place to live, get a dog or a cat or a tarantula, have a baby, have another. Next comes the minivan, a bigger house. And we'll be happy, right? That's the way it goes, isn't it?

What about those of us who can't afford a house when we first marry, or even when we're older and have children? What if we can't afford a sport utility vehicle like the Joneses?

And the big one: "Well, you have to do that job and stick with it, because you need to pay the bills." I have yet to hear anyone in a really excited voice say, "I just paid my hydro bill and I feel so fulfilled!"

We've been stuck in this current for so long, it must be right! *Wrong!*

In North America, more than half the marriages end in divorce. How many marriages that do survive are happy relationships? I have had friends say to me, "If my marriage dissolved for one reason or another, I would not do it again." And these statements are from people whose marriages appear to be sound.

How do broken marriages affect children? Parents spend less time with their kids than ever before. In Canada, in 1999, Kids Help Phone reported counseling more than eight hundred children every day. In Canada, more than 29 percent of women have been a victim of spousal assault. In the United States, the figure is 21 percent, and in Australia, 23 percent. How much of this is related to the fact that individuals and families are falling more into debt than ever before?

Getting a formal education is not necessarily a guarantee of a good life, although a quality education can enhance achievement. But there are other things needed, like discipline and persistence. There is a great quote by former U.S. president Calvin Coolidge on persistence: "The world is full of educated derelicts."

In the publication *Canadian Social Trends*, put out by Statistics Canada, an article makes this point: "between the

years of 1971 and 1996, the percentage of adults with more
than a high school education doubled from 21 percent to 50
percent." Are people more fulfilled now than in 1971?
Statistics prove otherwise. Approximately 22 percent of
university students feel that they are overqualified for the job
they are doing. Furthermore, some 23 percent of university
and community college graduates were employed in clerical,
sales or service jobs, which may not have required post-
secondary education. These people will feel frustration and
disappointment.

The truth is, we are sold on the idea that education equals a
job, and that the job *equals* fulfillment, which does not add up
for most of us. Education teaches us how to learn, and also
about the various functions of our world. This is to enhance our
lives, not necessarily get us a "job." When we take the approach
that education is a tool for improvement, then we can use it to
empower us, rather than limit us. The obvious point is that for
a great majority of people, their lives are not very fulfilled. We
are heading down this path and we've never really taken the
time to look at where we are or where we're going. The joke
about whoever has the most toys wins, is nothing more than
that. Trying to keep up with the other guy is never ending.

Ask yourself: "Would I take a train across the country if I
knew that somewhere along the way a bridge had collapsed
and the train would plunge into the river?" Of course not. Then
why are we doing it with something far more important like
our lives? We do it because we are stuck in this pattern of societal currents — the "Niagara Syndrome" — which makes us
feel guilty for doing what we love if no major monetary
rewards are attached or we are not doing all the other "things"
in our life we feel we *should* be doing.

As I said, this is my *view* of this structure, but it is to illus-
trate how other people and society's guidelines can have a

profound effect on an individual. Creating our own guidelines is essential for our long-term fulfillment. Technological examples of today show there are no longer any limits; what we believed was impossible is becoming possible. (Paraplegics on the cusp of walking again.)

If *you* are not satisfied, passionate and excited about your life, then how are the other things that come into your life, like a car, relationships, activities, and so on, be served with satisfaction, passion and excitement? They can't be. We have this illusion that these "things" will make us complete and happy. They don't. What we do as *individuals* on a daily basis is the basis for our fulfillment. A marriage and a host of other important things can bring us happiness, but only for a short while, if we are not excited about our own existence and the day that lies ahead.

We need to do an activity on a regular basis that excites us — I mean really excites us. It could be our job, which I call a "money activity." Doesn't that sound better? A MONEY ACTIVITY. For a lot of us, when we think of the word *job*, we tend to attach negative feelings to it. How do you think TGIF (Thank God It's Friday) became so popular? "Can't wait for Friday to get out of this crappy job!" I always found that kind of funny, because when you asked someone how their weekend was, they would respond by saying in a quiet sort of voice, "It was okay." or "Didn't do much, you know, painted the house, mowed the lawn." These are the same people who couldn't wait for Friday to come!

How about TGIM (Thank Gosh It's Monday). People would be looking at you like you fell off the train. If we can think of our "job" as a money activity, where we can socialize with others, learn and be creative, it may change our perspective and attitude a little . . . and you know what those motivational people say about attitude.

Now some of you will say, "Nothing gets me excited, really." But in every single one of us there is a passion, and we must take the time to find it, because when we do, our life will change. We can all do a great sales job when we are passionate about a subject.

Many people are afraid to go for what they want because in our society (another section in the current) we have been taught that aggressive and overly confident behavior can be obnoxious or hostile, or unfairly puts pressure on someone. And *we* don't want to portray that image! We just need to be assertive, not aggressive.

If you are currently involved with a situation and/or activity that brings you joy and excitement, and if someone puts you down because of it, either disconnect that person from your life or find a way to make them understand how important this is to you! It may be the person you are living with who is doing the belittling, and if so, you may be facing a very hard reality. If you stop doing the things that fulfill you, then everything else will fall apart at some point in your life — guaranteed!

To reiterate, we need to be excited, enthused, passionate, thrilled, ecstatic and stimulated with an activity first, before all other things and events in our lives can be enjoyed to their fullest.

COMPARTMENT 2

CULTIVATE YOUR
UNIQUENESS

Now that we are out of the current and *will not justify* to ourselves why we should go back in, it is important to understand what makes us *tick*. This compartment and the next one will deal with your own personality by aligning your mind and your heart along with your unique talents.

Your heart — that little pounding device in your body is there not only to keep the blood circulating, but it is there to guide you. Some of you may be thinking, *"It's there to what...?"*

Your heart can definitely guide you if you're willing to follow it. Think of the times you have told a lie, or have been late for some function, or have just plain let someone down.

Do a little test one day this week, because for most of us, that's all it will take. Next time you tell a little lie, or you are not very nice to someone, or you do not take the responsibility that you were supposed to, or are late for school or work, take notice of your heart. (I'm sure you really don't have to wait until next week; if you close your eyes and concentrate on previous incidents that were uncomfortable, you will get results immediately).

Also, take notice of your heart next time you are really nice to someone, finish a project on time that you are proud of, or when someone says how much they appreciate you. What is most amazing about this little test is that you get a totally different feeling from these two experiences. When you do something that is good, your heart will pound with excitement and joy. You may feel calm and at ease. When you do something that is not in line with your values, your heart will pound quickly, and you will feel tension, anxiety and maybe even fear.

So, if your heart tells the truth, then you know what direction is best for you to go in, and what direction is not. Our heart is our guiding light, and it guides us with precision. Some people call this intuition.

The point of the matter is that we have an internal gyroscope that needs to be tapped. Tapping into our heart is not a difficult process; we just have to pay attention to its direction and keep a log of our desires — what feels right and what does not and then act upon this feeling.

We must pay attention to how we feel and think about all the activities in our life. It's time to do something about the feelings and thoughts that will take us to where we ultimately want to go.

Unfortunately, many of us never get to the starting gate or really get in tune with our desires, as the musical group Pink Floyd wrote in their song "Time" from *Dark Side of the Moon*:

> You are young and life is long
> And there is time to kill today.
> And then one day you find ten years
> Have got behind you.
> No one told you when to run,
> You missed the starting gun.
> And you run to catch up with the sun,
> But it's sinking …
>
> But you're older, shorter of breath
> and one day closer to death!

That scares the *#@**# out of me. Those lyrics alone should make you want to go after the fulfillment you desire, immediately, before time runs out, *because it will.*

Our society is going through change and I think it is for the better, but we need to focus on ourselves to make us better. You can read all the books on finance and business and technology you want, but until you know yourself, those other tools may just lead to frustration.

And why is this? Because most of us do not take the time to think about what we really want! We have never been taught to do this, so this is no surprise. I am implementing a full unit in our education system that will teach young people this, but until then . . .

This tool could be called self-analysis, finding the real you, getting to know thyself, becoming one with my inner being, or we could just call it what it is: What do I want out of life and how do I get it? (See Exercises 3 and 4.) And the end result? Daily fulfillment and enhancing the lives of others!

Why should you be so concerned about enhancing the lives of others, and why do I mention it so often?

It is very important to attach your desires and goals to the betterment of others' lives, so that your accomplishments are not destructive to yourself or others. There are people who believe that selling drugs or running with a street gang or stealing is a great accomplishment. These destructive activities do damage and ruin lives.

And hurtful activities do not have to be illegal. They can be motivated by greed and a desire for control. Your desires must benefit your life and the lives of those around you. This will bring you peace of mind and fulfillment.

As well as being honest with ourselves, we must give to others, in a positive way and on a regular basis. There is a theory that some people believe in, and some don't, called the boom-a-rang theory. (Others call it "what you sow, so shall you reap," or "what goes around, comes around.") The people who do not believe in this idea generally don't because it's something they can't see, touch or smell. Can we see, touch or smell gravity? Of course not, but we know it is present. We drop an object and it falls to the ground, every time, without exception. It never drops halfway or three-quarters of the way to the ground, but always all the way. Even though we don't have any actual physical reference to this thing called gravity, it is a consistent force — just like the boom-a-rang theory.

THE BIG THREE AND HONESTY

All human beings want the same things. I call these "The Big Three":

1. To love and be loved
2. To be accepted
3. To feel good about ourselves

Unfortunately, few of us ever achieve The Big Three to their full potential. There are two main reasons for this. The first is lack of execution (which we will examine in greater detail) and second, and perhaps the most important reason we do not achieve The Big Three, is we are not honest with ourselves. Being totally honest about ourselves is a very scary proposition. Admitting our faults and weaknesses to others makes us feel vulnerable. But by admitting to our faults and weaknesses, we can bring others closer to us and get rid of all that harmful anxiety building up in us. We no longer have to defend who we are.

Here's an experiment to try. Ask someone you trust what

they think your faults are and what you can do to overcome them. You will get feedback you can use.

So the next time someone is judging you or giving you a hard time about who you are, say to that person, "You may be right. What do you think I can do about that?" Watch how all of a sudden their whole body language changes. They will have to step back and think about an answer that is positive. Chances are they will be tongue-tied and will immediately stop attacking you. Your question changes the situation completely.

To be honest with yourself you do not have to involve anyone else. You know by following your heart and by knowing what your shortcomings are, you can actively pursue a change that is enhancing — not debilitating.

Being totally honest will begin to bring out your own uniqueness and individuality, and will break down those barriers we put up that hold us back. We can do this by looking back at past events and learning from them, as well as decisions that made us feel uncomfortable at the time we made them (see Exercise 6). It may seem a little too simplistic, but over the years we slowly build up a wall that becomes a barrier to our potential. If we are totally honest with ourselves, we will find that endless possibilities are opened to us because the fear of failing will be eliminated and replaced with the excitement of possibilities. This happens because by being honest we have accepted who we are and now want to find ways of improving on a good thing!

The only way to get on the *road* to fulfillment and go on a *dream drive* with *honesty* as your vehicle is by asking yourself a few quality questions:

1. What is it about myself I want to improve? (Admit to yourself what must be improved.)

2. Do I serve my talents to the best of their abilities? (*Everyone* has talents.)
3. What is it about myself I dislike that holds me back from doing what is in my heart?
4. What is it that I do that I know is not right, and that affects my relationships with others?

There is a long list of questions you can ask yourself that will lead you to discovering your own personality. Asking good questions gets good answers! If you have enough courage, go to someone you trust and respect, and ask their opinion. Don't take their comments personally; look at it as a growth experience.

What you are trying achieve is to know and understand the root of some of your behaviors and feelings and actions. Our thoughts and the perception of what may come our way determine 99 percent of how we live. To achieve anything in life we must understand this and align ourselves in the direction that is best for ourselves. The fact of the matter is that we sometimes put on an image, pretend to be someone who we are not, or feel we have to be more than we are. This does not serve us well. Understanding yourself and being totally honest actually puts you in a position of strength, because never again, no matter what anyone says to you, will your mindset affect — your view of you.

If you are working hard to improve yourself and be honest — something we all have to do on a regular basis — then you're on your way to achieving fulfillment. Please don't accept your lot in life — life can *always be more rewarding*. Look at some of the people from around the world we see on television, in movies, on the Internet, or in the news who do fascinating things. They are no different than you and me. They have just taken their talents to the maximum.

Take your time to ask yourself the questions that will force you to be totally honest with yourself. I have a simple exercise you can try that will give you a very important tool. (See Exercise 1.)

The folk-rock group The Eagles wrote the following lyrics in a song called "Already Gone": "So often it happens that we live our lives in chains/ And never even know we had the key." The key is *honesty*.

USING OUR CIRCUMSTANCES TO OUR ADVANTAGE

Life is hard. Things happen to us that are outside of our control. You must find ways to understand the situation you're in and make responsible choices. (There's that CTC again!) Take control of your life! There are people out there you can trust and put your faith in.

If you are 19 years of age or younger, call your toll-free help line (1-800-668-6868 Canada). Someone will listen to your problem; they have no way of tracing your call. They will also give you additional resources so that you can get ongoing help if you want it or need it.

I hope that in the future we will have no need for a kids help phone, but for now we have to help kids who have suffered abuse or watched it happening in their homes. We must not let any incident "rape" us twice.

Some of you may be taken back by that statement, but we can no longer deny or hide from the fact that various acts hold us hostage and we must look at them for what they are and be strong to conquer them.

If you are over 19 years of age, look through your telephone book and find help groups, counselors or adult help lines. There is now one run by Kids Help Phone: 1-888-603-9100.

If you are a person who has committed abuse, get help immediately and then use your experience to stop others from doing the same.

The message here is that a majority of us has suffered a "dysfunctional" incident, and as much as we want to use it to justify our lack of accomplishments and fulfillment, that is only holding us back. It is defeating us. It is preventing us from growing, from moving forward.

Remember, take care of yourself first. Do not let anyone else's actions, words or guidelines stop you from having a fulfilled life. Don't let anger get the better of you, and never accept it as a way of forcing you to do something against your will.

Dealing with previous problems may make you realize how they are contributing to your present situation, and how you can use those situations to benefit you in the long run. Use Exercise 6, "Things I Have Survived," to help you see the strength you have and your ability to overcome obstacles.

With the tools in this book and the tools you will acquire along the way in life, you *will* find your fulfillment!

GETTING IN MOTION

Look around you. You'll see people who are doing what they love to do every day. These people have made decisions based on the resources available to them and followed *their* path. They might appear to be lucky, but the truth is they were prepared. So let's follow their examples and prepare for *our luck.*

The book *Uncommon Genius* by Denise Shekerjian uses as its perspective some of the winners of the MacArthur Award, on the subject of creativity. These are people from all walks of life who have and are still achieving great accomplishments.

There are common themes related to these individuals. Two of the common themes are 1) cultivate your talents over the long run, and 2) set up the necessary conditions to do your best work. By doing these things, one can freely enjoy the activity at hand without being concerned about *outcomes*. This also seems to produce a great deal of *luck*.

We may run into some opposition for the new direction we are going to take. There are some people who have the idea that not everyone can do what they like. That line of thinking has never made a lot of sense to me. People who think this way have been in the "current" too long. No matter what we do, we have to do research, learn new approaches, work hard, experiment, and take on challenges. If we have to do all of that, we might as well do it at an activity we enjoy. So, you might have to make some changes in your life.

No one likes change, but if we want our life to be more fulfilling, we have to change. I think people don't like change because they are afraid; perhaps they don't feel confident that the change will be good. But if change enhances our life and encompasses what we enjoy, change can be fun. What a concept!

Doing what we love to do on a regular basis will make us get up early in the morning and stay up late at night and keep our heart pounding in between times. What a wonderful ultimate destination. But, how do we know how to get there?

We may know what is in our heart, and what some of our talents are, but how do we transform our dreams and skills into a regular activity?

For some of you this is quite simple. You have had a hobby for years and this is what you love. For the rest of us who might not have a hobby or the innate physical talents that musicians and athletes possess, we have to *think* of how to transform our unique talents and passions into a regular activity.

We must take our time, regardless of our age, and take the necessary steps to achieve the fulfillment we desire. We must also enjoy the journey along the way. *No important decision has to be made quickly.* Please do not take this the wrong way. We have already wasted too much time and energy doing what we do not like, so we need to start the process immediately — just don't rush the process. I will tell you honestly, if you hook into something you like and start on your path to fulfillment, there will not be enough hours in the day.

Now that we have aligned our mind with our heart, it is time to *get in motion.* Remember, experiences (*in motion*) teach us how to gain knowledge and execute it, something briefly touched on at the beginning of the first compartment.

The key is, we must look back at previous experiences and evaluate them, and continue to have new ones and do the same.

For a young person, my advice would be to have a broad range of experiences up to the age of 25. Everything and anything (but remember *choices.* This is not to advocate anything harmful to you or anyone else). Seek out mentors who interest you and use their experiences to save you from pitfalls and mistakes. Then use the tools in this book and others to evaluate your unique talents and match them to your desires. Using this approach will put you on your way to daily fulfillment and accomplishing desired goals.

Without taking the time, without experimenting, experiencing and evaluating, how will you ever know what you might be missing?

If you don't take a chance, and try an experience you have read or heard about, how are you ever going to know what that experience is really like?

If you don't try to build that invention that's always been in the back of your head, how are you ever going to know the joy?

I had the interesting experience of operating a car wash at one time, but there was a slight problem: I didn't know much about fixing things. This was one of the "wash your own" car washes, which meant there was a fair amount of maintenance involved.

You see, my Dad and carpenter or plumbing tools didn't get along, so I was unaware these tools even existed. I used to hear him downstairs, yelling occasionally as he renovated the basement, even though he was the only one down there.

So here I am, on the first day as a car wash owner, with two employees — a big, burly guy and a tall, skinny one.

It was a freezing February day, and we had a leak 30 feet up on the roof. The floor was slanted and the ladder was rickety, and I am scared of heights. Well, about 10 minutes after *watching* these guys up the ladder trying to seal the leak, I was shaking from the cold. One of them said "Go inside before you get pneumonia." I could hear them laughing as I headed for warmth. I found out later they had a bet on how long I would last.

I did stay — for five years — and learned a great deal about running a business. I continue to use things I learned. For example, it taught me about organizational skills and the value of money.

I think the most important thing was the experience itself, and knowing that in a short time I was doing things I didn't believe I could.

I also had a small retail business in home décor, and learned a little about mail order, but more importantly, it reaffirmed some of my other talents. While running this business, I decided to teach people the art of stencilling. Of course, I never had done stencilling before, and I am partially colour blind, but I was just teaching others — not decorating their house. What this experience gave me was the discovery that I enjoyed organizing and putting on a seminar.

Only through one little experience after another, and by taking the time to evaluate those experiences, was I able to go on to the next with enthusiasm.

When you execute your knowledge by evaluating your experiences and recognizing your talents and match them up with an "Aligned Mind," your journey becomes limitless.

In case you are interested in starting your *own* business, after you have decided on what type of business you would like to be in, go to work for someone in that field and learn as much as you can. It may mean taking a part-time job to start, or even doing volunteer work, but the advantage is that you see the business as it is, before you take that uneducated leap into doing it as a committed owner. By doing this, you will be able to see things objectively without any real cost.

Before deciding to go into business for yourself, remember that you will end up doing a lot of things that are not exactly the things you like doing — accounting, selling, scheduling staff, etc. are all elements that a business owner takes responsibility for at the beginning, and possibly always. Owning a business is not the right situation for all of us. Becoming a partner in an existing firm is an option, along with many others. Once you have been in a field for a while, you will get to see the various options.

Many business owners say they would reconsider owning a business if they were given the opportunity to begin again. The reason is that there are so many skills business demands today, large or small, that it is almost impossible for one person to do it all themselves. Marketing, selling, accounting, scheduling, and research and development, among other aspects of running a business, are all the hats you will be required to wear. Business has progressed far beyond the previous generation, where one would acquire a product or service, place a few ads, send out a few promotional flyers, work hard, and be successful. Those days are long gone. Now, we must continually upgrade and try new things, or we will be left behind. So take it slow, learn from other people so that you reduce risk and increase your potential for fulfillment and pleasure.

Then, there are dreams — something that may take years to accomplish, something that only your imagination can see. Not everyone has dreams, and there is nothing wrong with that — we all have talents in different areas.

Can you be an expert in a particular field? Absolutely. Consistency is one of the keys. (As you can see, you will need a new "key chain.") Of course, recognizing your talents is a big help, too!

The reason consistency is a big key is that most people are not. The reason using your talent base to support your activity is important's, because most people do not. A lot of people think that because they watch or read the news, they are informed. To be properly informed, you must take what you hear and see in the media and then do some research. And how many people do that? Not many.

In other words, there is a whole lot of room for you to be an expert in any field that inspires you, if you are willing to be consistent over a period of time. Of course, this is a tough sell today with all of us wanting to achieve so quickly, or get there so quickly. We see people making large sums of money in real estate, the stock market or in the high-technology fields. These individuals who sustain this plateau are a speck of dust compared to those who lose heavily in all markets when trying to make money quickly and easily. The universal law of "cause and effect" always keeps things in order except for those specks of dust that get through every so often. Even the best vacuum cleaner in the world allows a few specks of dust to escape.

Most people are not willing to put in the time necessary to become the "expert" that will take them to new levels. It is more a matter of time than it is effort, slowly chipping away at the outside to learn more about what's inside. When we raise children, do we put them in the microwave like popcorn and expect them to ready in to take on the world in three and a half minutes? Learning is a consistent process over a long period of time. If you give sporadic stimuli you will get sporadic results.

Gaining fulfillment may have nothing to do with your "money activity." You may use that vehicle to take care of the necessities and another one that gives you your fulfillment. Whatever or wherever you get your fulfillment from, you will still have to experiment and evaluate until you get to your chosen destination. Only you will know if you feel peace of mind throughout the entire day, regardless of what gives you long-term fulfillment.

If you're on the road toward your desired destination, what could be better? Most of the time the journey is better than the destination itself! This may be hard to believe for some of you, but think of athletes *after* the championship game is over, or children *after* they open their Christmas presents. On the road, in motion, the *doing*, is the part that human beings have always excelled at. Whether you make it to your destination exactly when you want to, or if at all, is not the point. Taking the chance and learning along the way, which will present more opportunities, is what it is all about and where the fulfillment comes from.

Have you had one of those days when you said to yourself "That's it, I'm just not satisfied," then someone or something *settled* you down and you returned to work or think according to someone else's guidelines? *Settled*. Doesn't that word make you shiver? If it doesn't, make it. Rocks "settle" at the bottom of the ocean. Food "settles" at the bottom of the fish tank. You don't want to settle for just anything. We only have so much time. As Harold Taylor says in his book *Making Time Work For You*, "time, it's an irreplaceable resource. When time's gone, you're gone." We must enjoy our time and make sure we are fulfilled.

So the equation, or the cycle, for recognizing talent and executing knowledge is really quite simple.

$$E1+E2 = GK \& RT$$
$$GK+T+DA=EK$$

Experimenting (1) – Evaluating (2) = Gained Knowledge & Recognized Talent

Gained Knowledge + Talents + Desired Activity = Executed Knowledge

In essence, the art of executing knowledge is the art of experimenting and evaluating, then taking that knowledge and aligning it with our desired activity. We must take the time to understand how we can get the most out of what we have. We must understand that taking the time to evaluate our experiences on a consistent basis will save time and frustration in the future, and give us great insight. We tend not to push ourselves to find out what we are capable of doing. Many of us were never taught the process of experimenting and evaluating in conjunction with *our own* talents. We get into the real world and find out that we need another set of tools than the ones we are provided with through our formal education.

Taking the time is one of the more important elements. As

difficult as it may be to realize, taking time to evaluate what we do will actually save time and lead to much more rewarding results. How many of us spend more time and are more excited about planning our trip to a Florida beach than we do planning our life? A two-week trip lasts for 336 hours. The rest of the year has 8,424 hours in it. Which deserves more planning and evaluating?

I will not sell you the line that it is a quick fix, because it is not. If anyone tells you, or tries to sell you on anything in regards to being able to obtain your dreams and gain long-term fulfillment in a short time frame, walk away. (A good *choice*.) We are all different and what will take me a couple of hours to accomplish may take you only an hour. Go at your own pace, enjoy the journey, and choose the direction.

Going at your own pace does not give you an excuse to say, "Well, I went at my own pace and nothing happened — where is that TV remote control?" You must get and stay in motion on a consistent basis, and make sure you don't settle like sediment at the bottom of a river. Anything in motion gathers more speed as it goes along. Think of a snowboarder racing downhill, out of control!

We need tangible tools to help us go in the direction we want to pursue. One of the biggest mistakes we make is not taking the time to write down *previous* experiences and evaluate them, or taking the time to evaluate our skills, strengths and weaknesses. (See Exercise 8.) Whether it is a money activity, a hobby or a dream from which you will draw your daily and constant fulfillment, the process is the same.

I have had a certain remark come my way several times.

"I don't have any experiences." (You're talking and walking, aren't you?)

We all have experiences and passions.

"But I don't want to experiment!"

There is nothing I can do about the lack of someone's will. If you don't want to experiment, then don't justify. Don't lay the blame on anyone else. Remember what was said about circumstances. If you work through the Eleven Exercises, which will not take long, you will find that you will *want to experiment*!

The choice is yours — to get in motion or not!

I learned some interesting facts from one of my favorite books, *Uncommon Genius*, about conditions.

Did you know that the philosopher Emmanual Kant wrote while in bed at the same time every day, staring at a tower out his window. When the trees grew too big and blocked his view, he had them cut down.

Or Charles Dickens, who always made sure his bed faced north, believing he was enabled by magnetic forces.

The composer Beethoven stimulated his mind by pouring ice-cold water over his head.

Personally, I just like a quiet room to work in. Sometimes, upbeat music or long walks in the country can also do it for me.

Whatever the conditions are that get you in motion and keep you stimulated create them, be in them constantly — they will make a difference.

MAPPING IT OUT

Going for a drive is a wonderful analogy about how obstacles get in our way and how we can manage to stay calm and find ways around them. Think about when you go for a drive, and you get to an intersection when the light is red. You stop. You don't ignore the light and drive through the intersection, dodging cars as you go. You don't pull out your sling shot and shoot the red light. You don't get out of your car and jump up and down and scream and . . . (If you do any of these things, please don't come to my neighborhood). You wait until the light turns green and then you go on your way.

On your drive to a friend's house or wherever you are going, by car or bus, you may have to stop at every red light and wait. Other times you steer clear of the majority of red lights and you get to your destination much sooner. That's life in a nutshell. (Who thought up that saying, anyway?). The difference between those who make our way to our destination in life and those who wander aimlessly and JUSTIFY, JUSTIFY, JUSTIFY is a *map*! You will never find your friend's house, your workplace, the pizza parlor, the shoe store, the golf store or the Christmas tree farm, unless you have a map to show you how to get there the first time you go. (For some of us, we need it for more than just the first time!) Most importantly, the map gives you direction, so the obstacles are just a challenge and not a wall that you cannot get past.

Think of a time when you took a long driving trip. A map *guides* you in the direction you want to go. Sometimes it is a scenic drive or sometimes you just want to get there as fast as you can. The point is that without that map, chances are you may never get to your destination.

Do you have a map for your life? If you do not, then how do you expect to ever go where you really want to go and experience all of the things that you have the ability to experience? The frightening thing is, most of us do not have a map for our life, but we complain when things do not work out, or that we do not live our lives with passion and fulfillment.

Decide on your heart's desire, and make a *map* (see Exercise 10) of how to get there. Remember there may be construction on some of the roads, so you may have to take a detour. When you get to a red light, stop, think calmly, wait, and then continue on your road. As long as you have a map, you know you will make it, it is just a matter of time. Make it a DREAM DRIVE ON YOUR DREAM ROAD TO FULFILL-MENT!

CREATING A ROUTINE

Our days go by very fast because of all the different activities that we are involved in. It is very easy for a month, a year, even a decade to go by without accomplishing what we really wanted to. The main reason for not accomplishing all that we want to is that we dont take the time to create a routine (see Exercise 11) and schedule the activities that will help us on our journey. Many times we tend to say "Oh yeah, I'll get to that" and then never do.

We have many distractions in this fast-paced world of ours, and the only way to accomplish what we want is to create a routine and schedule in what is necessary. Some people do not like to have a routine or a schedule; they say it is too struc-tured. But creating a routine and doing a schedule actually gives you more flexibility, or as a friend of mine calls it, "Organized freedom!"

Most of us have "To Do" lists that we work from, but it is *how* we work from them that makes the difference. Take items from your "To Do" list and schedule them into your daily planner to make sure you actually *do* them. Many of us are just good list makers!

We all have certain tasks we must do on a daily or weekly basis. Then there are the ones we don't *really* need to do, but we get enjoyment out of doing them. Of course, there are a lot of time-wasters too. And we have those items that we need to do if we want to get that level of fulfillment we desire.

First, schedule the routine items (i.e., physical exercise,

part-time work, pay bills, eat, school, etc.), and then the "To Do" items (i.e., rollerblading, go shopping, plan vacation, party, learn about my desired activity, etc.) onto your daily calendar. Your "To Do" list must include the things you need *to do* to create your "fulfilling activity." Eventually, or possibly immediately, your *activity* will become a regular routine.

Schedule a whole month ahead including all the other activities that are part of your life. At the end of the month, spend a couple of hours on a quiet evening to evaluate the previous month and schedule the next month. Some things in the current month will work and some will not. But you will do and experience much more using this method than by trying to fit your items in "when you get a chance." Those chances never amount to much. Don't give anything up that is really important to you — just figure out how you can schedule it to make it part of your life. This is part of the evaluating process.

I know this appears very simple, but most of us do not take the simple actions of thinking and designing. To be in control of your life you have to take control. The better you schedule and stick by your routine, the more of life's experience will be yours.

And the more you experience, the more you will enhance your life and those of people around you.

To get an interesting perspective and to discover some useful tools on time management, read Harold Taylor's book *Making Time Work For You*. (See the "More Tools" section.)

CREATE YOUR OWN "BIO"

WHY A BIO IS A GOOD TOOL

This is the compartment where the cultivation process really begins by planting your foundation's seeds. Do not settle for a destination you don't want and an outcome you have not designed.

Exercises and templates are here to help you create your own "bio" (a journal of your life; a retrospective, a projection of where you want to go, your skills, your experiences, etc.), to get you in motion and stay in motion. The purpose of these exercises, as mentioned before, is to get you to think and evaluate your situation. By doing this you will come up with ideas that will give you more opportunities and choices while traveling along your path.

The "bio" is also a good tool if you suffer from depression to any degree. It will be something to view or study, to show you that things are possible. One other note about depression; if you experience it, don't fight it. When it occurs, accept it and tell yourself it will pass. Seek medical assistance if you require it, but my point is that we tend to fight depression as opposed to acknowledging that it is part of our lives from time to time, and we need to tell ourselves that we will not let this control our behavior.

There are some very important pages to follow, some of which talk about how to set goals, create an action plan, and put new guidelines into place, as well as many other things. The exercises have been simplified so that you do not have to spend more time reading them than acting on them. This section has been designed to help you complete these exercises. The more you put into the exercises, the more you will benefit from them. You must think and write down what reflects who you are — not someone else.

You may at times get a little frustrated while compiling information to create your "bio," but please remember why you are doing this, keep focused and patient, and have a little *trust*. Once it is completed you will have an inspiring piece of work that will be fulfilling in itself and will be another tool to help in your quest for fulfillment.

Each exercise describes what needs to be done along with examples on one page, followed by a blank page for you to fill out. Take your time and enjoy the process.

You can do the actual exercises right in the book, but I suggest that you get a three-ring binder with lined paper and keep that binder as your "bio." You can also do it on the computer and then print the pages out and put them the binder.

Read all of the exercises before starting the first to get a sense of what you need to do.

THE ELEVEN EXERCISES

Get the necessary tools for the purpose of recognizing your talents and executing your knowledge to bring achievement and fulfillment. Enhance your life & the ones that surround you and go on an exhilarating journey.

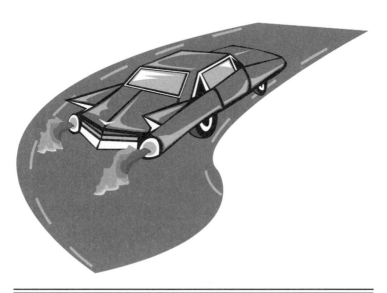

EXERCISE 1: **HONESTY**

This will review some things we talked about in Compartment 2. It is important to keep all of your "bio" together for easy review.

Being honest is the first important step to take you to fulfillment. You may have other questions that can be added to this list — the more the better.

When I look back upon my life, what do I want to have accomplished, contributed to, been part of, experienced and learned?

_____

_____

_____

_____

What is it about myself that I want to improve? (Admit to yourself what must be improved.)

_____

_____

_____

_____

What can I do to use my talents to the best of my ability?

_____

_____

_____

_____

What is it about myself that holds me back from doing what is in my heart?

_____

_____

_____

_____

What is it that I do that affects my relationships with others (good and bad)?

_____

_____

_____

_____

How would you act if you were fulfilled?

How would you act if you were not fulfilled?

EXERCISE 2: **HOW WOULD I ACT AND NOT ACT IF I WAS FULFILLED?**

This exercise will help determine how aligned you are in your quest for fulfillment. The following are some examples.

ACT	NOT ACT
Be happy and cheerful	Negative comments about others
Positive actions	Negative actions
Balance: - peace of mind	Get angry
- enjoy quiet times	Get frustrated
- engage challenge	Argue relentlessly
- keep learning	Do destructive things
- maintain good relationships	Be jealous
Look at the positive in all situations	Worry about what other people think
"What did I learn today?"	
Talk only about people's positive attributes	

ACT	NOT ACT

*Do not be a sheep,
unless you are
the lead sheep
in your life ...*

*Otherwise, the
scenery never
changes ...*

EXERCISE 3: **WHAT I WANT OUT OF LIFE**

Along with the exercise on honesty, this exercise is important because we need to know exactly what we want. This is in general terms only. You will get more specific in upcoming exercises..

The following is an example of statements to help complete this exercise.

1. I want to enjoy every minute of every day. *I WILL.*
2. To accomplish this I must not react to situations. I know that any situaton can be dealt with. Just look at the past. Do not take anything too seriously, though work at it as if it is. *I WILL.*
3. I want to spend my leisure time with fabulous, fun and enthusiastic people. I want to do fun, creative and inspiring things with people. I want my relationships to have respect, love, understanding and above all communication in all aspects. *I WILL.*
4. I want to learn as much as possible. *I WILL.*
5. I want to experience as much as possible. *I WILL.*
6. I want to get along with as many people as possible. *I WILL.*
7. I want to travel the world. *I WILL.*
8. I want to own an entertainment business that enhances people's lives, as well as entertains them. *I WILL.*
9. I want to volunteer to enhance other people's lives as well as mine. *I WILL.*
10. I want to live in a house in the country. *I WILL.*
11. At the end of my life each "want" will have this written beside it — *I HAVE.*

DEFINITION OF WILL: The mental faculty by which a person decides to control his or her own actions. This is accomplished through determination: a person's attitude that can influence or compel to action. To get what one desires.

WHAT I WANT OUT OF LIFE

Separate the areas of your life that are the most important. Follow the examples on the previous page. Be demanding on yourself, and create a vision that you want to aspire to.

_____
_____
_____
_____
_____
_____
_____
_____
_____
_____
_____
_____
_____
_____
_____
_____
_____
_____
_____
_____
_____
_____
_____
_____

C T C

(No, not KFC — hang in there!)

COURAGE … to follow your visions.

TRUST … in your abilities.

CHOICES … that will give you a better today.

EXERCISE 4: **HOW TO GET WHAT I WANT OUT OF LIFE**

You now need a follow-up on how to get to your destination. This is called "What I want out of life." Will I take a vehicle in good running order, or will I take a 1970 "Pacer"? (An old funny-looking car that resembled the first space shuttle.) Push yourself a little to make sure you get to your destination. Always continue to think of ways to improve to make this journey fun.

Don't be concerned about an image you have to create for others; follow your heart, create a vision. Sometimes we feel we have to protect our image. We feel we need to put up walls to keep people from discovering our imperfections and penetrating our inner vulnerabilities. *Who cares?* Think for just one minute. As individuals, we are a microcosm of this planet, a little ant on the grass in the park. Who are we trying to protect ourselves from — another ant? You have the *choice* to let your humor out and act silly, and if someone else finds your behavior strange, they can tell their other ant friends!

Keep things in perspective. We are here for a very short time and the people we meet are a blink in time over the course of time. You have no inner weakness, just an inner light that needs to shine through those walls. Go ahead — make someone look at you today and wonder — maybe you will make them smile.

Sorry, I went a little off-track there! Let's return to our exercise on how to accomplish what you want out of life.

The following are some examples to support your vision.

I will:
- Listen to and read inspirational material from all sources.
- Not let other people's poor attitude affect mine.
- Have integrity and strive for honesty.
- Not talk about other people in a negative manner.
- Work hard.
- Go out of my way for others; do more than what is expected of me.
- Excercise on a regular basis.
- Eat well.
- Listen to others: don't think about what I want to say.
- Find role models.
- Always re-evaluate.
- Never be afraid to fail.
- Be kind to other people.
- Be personable.
- Always volunteer in some way.
- Always try new things.
- Read my "bio" every day.

HOW TO GET THERE

It is important to have a mission statement, outline, map, etc., but you need a vehicle to take you there in order to reap the benefits and realize your goals and dreams. Again, follow the previous examples that relate to the exercise and make the "HOW" a road that will take you to the "WHAT."

_____
_____
_____
_____
_____
_____
_____
_____
_____
_____
_____
_____
_____
_____
_____
_____
_____
_____
_____
_____
_____
_____
_____
_____
_____
_____
_____
_____
_____

JUSTIFY
JUSTIFY
JUSTIFY

THE HUMAN EXPERIENCE

"Ah, one more missed test, what's the big deal. . . . It's okay, I'll do the one next Tuesday, June 2, because I hear it's a good month and the right day to do a test because it's a new moon. Besides, I'm only 19 and grade 11 will still be here next year. Last night was a night I couldn't miss, chatting on the Internet to someone who lives in Japan — cool — and . . .

EXERCISE 5: **GUIDELINES AND JUSTIFYING**

This is a major part of your "bio"! Having *your own* guidelines is very important. You won't get what you want out of life if you follow other people's guidelines.

We tend to think and respond the same way that people who surround us on a regular basis do, and we need to separate our own pattern of thinking from what theirs may be. These people include our parents, friends, mentors, religious associates and others who have a profound effect on our lives. Unfortunately, we tend to pick up on some of *their* guidelines, which they picked up from someone else. As we know, a significant number of people are not fulfilled. Do we want their guidelines for our lives? I don't think so. We tend to create guidelines that stop us from ever being fulfilled, and this means we will be continuously frustrated.

For instance, my guidelines for basic fulfillment used to be (before I really sat down and thought about them) that I had to accomplish everything I set out to do and *nothing* could stop me. If I was not constantly making *more* money every year or winning all the time, or making sure that *every* project was hassle-free, or striving to make *every* moment in my intimate relationships a moment of absolute bliss and happiness, I must be unfulfilled. Chances are, with the attitude I had, I was going to be unfulfilled before I even started. The purpose of creating your own guidelines, then, is to make it easy to achieve and difficult not to.

Creating your own guidelines will take some time on your part and perhaps some time spent with friends, along with some real *honesty*. I held a session with a couple of different groups of friends and had them analyze me. If you are going to do this, you *must* promise yourself that you will not take their responses personally, but use them as a means of improving yourself.

While doing the guideline exercise, cover up the examples at first, and write down what your guidelines are in your life, at present, for each heading. Then study your current guidelines and think about how they may stop you from achieving *what you want*. After completing these sequential steps, look at my guidelines for each one. Compose your own guidelines to simplify and enrich your lifelong journey.

The following is a list of guidelines that may be useful. You will probably have different categories and possibly many more. The "Justifiers" are things you will not allow yourself to use to keep you from following your desire.

FOR BASIC FULFILLMENT:
- I must do something every day to make myself a better person (volunteer, read, listen to inspirational people, do, do, do).
- I must never give up on my journey.

FOR FRIENDS:
- I will enjoy their company
- I will be thankful for all my relationships.

FOR MY SPECIAL RELATIONSHIP:
- I must first choose a partner who inspires me and has the same values (make sure you know what inspires you!)
- I will make my partner laugh at least once a day.
- I will give unconditionally.

FOR BUSINESS/SCHOOL:
- I will help others feel good about using the product or service where I work.
- I will serve people to the best of my ability without expecting anything in return.

FOR MY PHYSICAL WELL-BEING:
- I must work out on a regular basis.
- I will be disciplined in my eating habits.
- I must not consume things that are harmful to my body.

FOR MY MENTAL WELL-BEING:
- I will live by my guidelines and values and beliefs.
- I will be thankful for what I have been a part of and accomplished.
- I will read my "bio" on a regular basis.

JUSTIFIERS

I don't know how.	I am not able to.
I will do it as soon as . . .	I can't find any information on . . .
I'll do it next month.	Other people tell me not to.

MY GUIDELINES

The previous introduction to guidelines explained the purpose for building this solid foundation of principles. This is one of the most important exercises to do for the fulfillment and peace of mind. Add categories to suit yourself.

BASIC FULFILLMENT:

_____

_____

_____

_____

_____

SPECIAL RELATIONSHIP:

_____
_____
_____
_____
_____
_____

MENTAL WELL-BEING:

_____
_____
_____
_____
_____
_____

FRIENDS:

_____
_____
_____
_____
_____
_____

HAPPINESS:

_____
_____
_____
_____
_____

THINGS THAT I HAVE SURVIVED

AND SOME THAT OTHER PEOPLE HAVE, TOO.

EXERCISE 6: **THINGS I HAVE SURVIVED**

In my opinion, one of the hardest and most challenging obstacles in life is being able to see the light at the end of the tunnel, especially when we are in a situation we don't want to be in. We need to know that we are making progress and that we will get to the next step on our ladder of fulfillment. This is the reason we need to keep a list of some of the things we have a lived through. These do not have to be earth-shaking events: they may include anything we did that seemed to be never ending, that we thought we would never get through — but did! These feelings happen to all of us; the difference is how we deal with the situation. Doing the following exercise puts future situations in perspective.

The following is a list of events that you may have lived through and may trigger some other events you may have forgotten about.

The long school years

Years of hard work and long hours put into a business only to lose it due to a chain of events that you could not control

The loss of a relationship with a partner with whom you could not connect

The theft of personal items

Friendships lost

The death of someone close

The loss of a job

A massive fire

Years without much money

Being assaulted

The loss of a pet

It is essential to acknowledge to yourself the hurdles you have overcome and survived, to realize that you have the ability and the strength to persevere regardless of the adversities. Everything can be overcome; it all depends on when you decide to overcome a situation and get ready to take action. If you are having a hard time trying to overcome something, look at your list and decide to act now! Look at someone else's list and you may wonder why you were even worrying in the first place. Remember to keep things in perspective.

Do you have trouble seeing the light at the end of the tunnel, while you are working towards something? Do obstacles seem too big? Do you get frustrated when it appears you will not overcome an overwhelming task? Of course you do. 🙂 We all do. What, then, makes some carry on, while others give up? Some of us suffer from "p.p."— puny perspective! We forget the times when we made it through tough events. We forget all the other people that do not have it half as easy as we do.

So release your "p.p." and get some relief from looking at the events you have made it through!

EXERCISE 7: **PERSPECTIVE**

This is a quick but very important exercise. Write down stories and events about people who are in life situations worse than your own, and about people who have overcome obstacles and achieved great things. Always add to this list when a story comes your way that will give you perspective on your own life. (Watching the news or reading the papers can do this very quickly).

HEADLINE (Main point of story to help you remember)

FULL STORY

HEADLINE (Main point of story to help you remember)

_____

FULL STORY

_____
_____
_____
_____
_____
_____
_____
_____
_____
_____
_____

HEADLINE (Main point of story to help you remember)

_____

FULL STORY

_____
_____
_____
_____
_____
_____
_____
_____
_____
_____

"THE BIG THREE"

TO LOVE AND BE LOVED

TO BE ACCEPTED

TO FEEL GOOD ABOUT OURSELVES

EXERCISE 8: **PREVIOUS EXPERIENCE AND RECOGNIZING TALENTS**

This is where the first part of the equation "recognizing talents and executing knowledge" comes into play.

To some of you, this exercise may appear to be a difficult one, if you believe that you do not have many talents due to not having done a variety of activities. This is a false belief. If you are more than ten years old, there are a lot of talents you have put to use. The difficult part may be actually picking out those talents you have been using. Take an inventory of everything you have done or thought about doing since you can remember — everything —and I guarantee that when you look close enough you will see a pattern of talents.

Please take your time with this and continue coming back to this exercise as you go through the cycle of experiences throughout your life. Remember that you must always take an inventory and re-evaluate, no less than twice a year.

To finish off the equation of "recognizing talents and executing knowledge," you have to match the talents that have emerged with your desires to *execute that knowledge.* You will do just that in the next exercise.

Here is a list of talents and where they were put to use:

The talents of:
   organizing
   producing
   creating
   being resourceful

Found in these activities:

> putting together electronic components
> paper route
> putting together school yearbook
> sports teams
> putting together events and parties
> setting up classes, seminars and workshops
> shooting videos

These are only a few examples. Think of all the experiences you have had, and write down the talents you need to execute that activity.

MY PREVIOUS EXPERIENCES AND RECOGNIZING TALENTS

Previous experience: _____

_____

_____

What I enjoyed/Talents used: _____

_____

_____

_____

Previous experience: _____

_____

_____

What I enjoyed/Talents used: _____

_____

_____

_____

Previous experience: _____

_____

_____

What I enjoyed/Talents used: _____

_____

_____

_____

Previous experience: _____

_____

_____

What I enjoyed/Talents used: _____

_____

_____

_____

Previous experience: _____

_____

_____

What I enjoyed/Talents used: _____

_____

_____

_____

LIST OF TALENTS

_____

_____

_____

_____
_____
_____
_____
_____
_____
_____
_____
_____
_____
_____
_____
_____
_____
_____
_____
_____
_____
_____
_____
_____
_____

IS *YOUR* "MONEY ACTIVITY" TAKING
YOU DOWN *YOUR* ROAD TO
FULFILLMENT?

DO YOU HAVE ALL THE NECESSARY
"TOOLS" IN PLACE TO GET ON YOUR
ROAD AND STAY ON IT?

EXERCISE 9: **DESIRE, VISION AND MISSIONS**

This exercise and the next one complete the second half of the equation of "recognizing talents and executing knowledge." They are about how to execute your knowledge. You now need to take your list of talents along with all the other exercises and match them to your desires. Then you need to create vision and mission statements. These statements are what you are about, and what you plan to do. You need to create a focus, that gyroscope. As time goes on, you will probably adjust these statements. But to be on the journey of achievement and fulfillment, you must know and be confident in your direction.

Your vision and mission statement must be short and concise. Use only one or two lines. When I did these statements myself, I thought they should be long, but the focus gets lost and makes the statements hard to remember. You want something that will guide you and move you forward, based on the previous exercises.

The vision statement is a view of who you are. Your vision statement could be something like "Energizing the Enterprise."

The mission statement is what you are going to do to make the vision statement a reality. For example, your mission statement could be "Eliminating preconceived notions and willing to use my unique talents through unlimited experiences."

As with all these exercises, it is important to take the time to complete this one in full. When you are done, you will have a unique outline of yourself — an outline that very few people ever set out to do, thus accounting for a lack of direction and accomplishment with fulfillment.

You may have more than one desire – fantastic! Just ensure you do Exercises 9 and 10 for each one. Exercise 10 will be the making of your map, where you will put your desire, vision and mission on the road.

MY DESIRE, VISION AND MISSION STATEMENTS

My Desire: _____

_____

_____

_____

Vision Statement: _____

_____

_____

_____

Mission Statement: _____

_____

_____

_____

_____

_____

_____

_____

_____

_____

_____

_____

_____

_____

_____

_____

_____

_____

The S&F virus
(success and failure)

is everywhere!

Make sure you get vaccinated.

EXERCISE 10: **MAKING A MAP AND CREATING CONDITIONS**

It is time to make a plan, create the map. This can be and probably will be altered during the journey. Without it, you will be driving aimlessly. If you were traveling and your destination was Calgary, Alberta, obviously you would need a map of Canada. A map of Australia would send you a little off the path!

If you are not 100 percent sure at this point of all the different aspects of your plan, that's okay; start it off and add to it as you go along, and stay in motion.

The "Why" and "How" sections in this exercise are very important, because they will push you and direct you. Make sure you give yourself lots of reasons *why* you want to go in a certain direction, because this will motivate you and support your decision.

There were many destinations I had a desire to go to. After following my map, I found these "destinations" were not as they appeared to be from the outset. So I stopped and looked at the other destinations my heart desired and that my talents supported, and started up again. I hope the first "destination" you're going to travel to is right for you, but it may not be. Don't give up. Re-think your situation and pick another destination and go for it. If you go through this process enough times, you will find the right destination and the fulfillment you desire. You will probably be fulfilled on the journey even if the destination you reach doesn't turn out to be what you expected.

Remember the example of Thomas Edison who worked on ten thousand experiments before accomplishing his desire. When asked what he'd be doing if he hadn't reached his desired goal, he said "I'd be working on ten thousand and one!"

Also remember how important the surrounding conditions are and try to set up the ones that keep you motivated.

Here is a sample of a destination and how to reach it.

DESTINATION: Become an editor in the video/movie business.
Why I want to go there:

- I love being able to put pieces of film together and create a finished product.
- I love adding music to scenes to create different dimensions of sound.
- I love my work to be entertaining.
- I love to use my skills.
- I love to take a vision and make it a reality.

PAST EXPERIENCE:

- Taken many courses.
- Read many books on the subject.
- Spent hours shooting and editing movies as a hobby.

HOW TO GET TO MY DESTINATION:

- Do volunteer work.
- Get involved with related associations.
- Ask people in those associations about opportunities.
- Gather information by calling and searching the Internet for companies that are in the movie/video business.
- Get employed at any level in this industry and learn while I am there how to get to my destination.

CONDITIONS I NEED:

- Listen to inspiring music.
- Go for long drives or long walks in the country.
- Work out at the gym.

MY MAP AND CONDITIONS
MY DESTINATION:

My Destination:_____

_____

_____

_____

_____

Why I Want To Go There: _____

_____

_____

_____

_____

Past Experiences: (If any): _____

_____

_____

_____

_____

How To Get To My Destination: _____

_____

_____

_____

_____

Conditions: _____

_____

_____

_____

_____

FOLLOW YOUR HEART …

BECAUSE YOU CAN
NEVER
FOOL YOUR HEART.

WITHOUT A FOCUSED "I,"
IT IS IMPOSSIBLE TO SEE.

EXERCISE 11: **CREATE A ROUTINE**

To get the most out of your time, it is very important to *design your time.*

Insert activities from your "To Do" list along with your "Routine" activities onto your calendar for the next month. Evaluate at the end of the month. (Re-read Compartment 2: Creating a routine to do this properly.)

MY "TO DO" LIST	MY ROUTINE ITEMS

CONGRATULATIONS!

You have completed all exercises in this section!

Now you have your own personal "BIO"!

Do an inventory and readjust your "BIO"
as you go to keep focused — *no less than
every six months.*

PUT YOUR TOOLS TO WORK

It can be difficult to acquire information about people, places, organizations, products, etc., so that we can make informed choices. It appears easy from the outside looking in — all we have to do is telephone people and organizations, right?

It is true that we have to make contact and "network" with people, but for some of us this is not as easy as it appears. We need to be prepared in order to start networking and gathering information. You are already more prepared than most because you have created your own "bio," but there still is a little more work to be done.

In the book *Great Connections*, which is about communicating, the authors Anne Baber and Lynne Waymon advise people to always set an agenda before going to any function or before making contact with someone. An agenda, in this case, is a list or an outline of ideas that you can share information about. Both giving and receiving. This is a great tool for gathering information.

Before making contact, create an agenda using the following information and write down some questions you might have based on the knowledge and research you've done. With the Internet and other sources of information, it has become relatively easy to get information about most things. What a great time we live in because we can *use* these new resources available to us instead of being *used up* with frustration and feeling overwhelmed.

The only difference between the people you hear about or know personally, who have accomplished a great deal and are fulfilled and the people who have not, is that those who do achieve knew what they wanted and prepared themselves to go after it. Nothing more, nothing less.

You already know your talents and skills based on your own "bio." It is time to prepare yourself for that *luck*.

GATHERING INFORMATION

We need to know how to gather the information we need in relation to what we want to be involved in. The great thing about "information gathering" is that sometimes you'll discover things about a particular subject you do not like — things you did not know before. *"What is so great about that?"* you might ask. Well, I was researching an industry that I really wanted to get involved in, only to discover that a lot of people in that industry did not reflect my beliefs and values. It would have been a huge waste of time if I had spent three years in an educational course, and then spent a few more years in the industry, only to find out that it was not at all what I had hoped for. This is why information gathering is very critical to your ultimate goal of fulfillment. Going through this process will take you in directions you may never have thought of. Therefore, stay committed. The information and knowledge you collect will reveal more than you expect.

I will say this again: take your time. This research does not have to be done in short time frame. This may sound unconventional, but I enjoy the researching and talking to people as much as the end result, and you may, too.

> A great source for you to gather information and share information is the website "Taking IT Global."
> **www.takingitglobal.org**

Start by creating a short personal statement in relation to the subject you are gathering information about and put this in your "bio" binder. Use the information in your bio to create this statement. Keep this handy while doing your information searching and gathering. Use the following example as a guide.

Example of personal statements if you were interested in the event industry.

- I have experience in organizing, planning and executing events through volunteer and paid positions.

- I enjoy creating and co-ordinating events (use past experiences to show skills used):
  – planning and executing parties, volunteer events, etc.
  – organizational skills, resourcefulness, etc.

- I believe the combination of my creativity along with my limitless energy to bring together interesting events that serve people in interesting ways.

- With my skills and my experiences, I believe I am a valuable asset for a cause, company, project or organization.

- I do my best work with short, intense projects.

If you have no experience, make a list of the talents and skills required by an activity that interests you. This will enhance your chances of getting involved with such an activity.

SCRIPTS AND QUESTION SHEET

The following few pages are "scripts" to help you gather the information. Modify them according to your style and situation, as these are guidelines to enhance your search for knowledge. As you go along, try to cancel any emotions of apprehension or intimidation concerning the person on the other end of the phone, or in front of you. Remember that they had to do exactly what you are doing to have achieved their current position. While soliciting information over the telephone, if you need to use the old "I am calling on behalf of a friend" routine at first to become familiar and comfortable with this process, do it. Keep in mind that people are very busy and occasionally have bad days. These scripts can be used for your money activity, your hobby, volunteering, or for your dream.

In following these or any scripts (that you will be repeating many times over in succession), the key is to speak as enthusiastically the hundredth time as you did the first. Smile when you make the call; you can hear the difference in your voice.

You must be persistent and patient, and realize that it will take many different contacts to get information. Never forget why you are doing this. It's for *you* — so that you can do an activity on a regular basis and achieve fulfillment. Enjoy opening your presents.

Read through the whole script section before starting to use it.

COLD-CALLING AN ORGANIZATION

- Hello, how are you? (Be sincere but not too serious.)

- My name is _____. I am interested in (the subject you are gathering information about) and I am looking for someone who can share some key points or information about the subject. Who would be best to talk to about this in your organization?
  Thank you for your assistance.

When you reach that person:

- Hello, how are you? (Be sincere but not too serious.)

- My name is _____. I am interested in (the subject you are gathering information about) and I am looking for someone who can share some key points or information about the subject. The person (use name if you have it) at the switchboard gave me your name and said you may be able to help me. Would this be a suitable time for you to answer a few questions? Is there a time I could try calling back?

Listen to the response.
Have your question sheet ready.

When calling an organization when you have the name of the person you want to speak to, choose one of the following:

1. **Through an association or article you've read, etc.**
   (If you are a member of that organization, let them know.)

- Hello, is _____ there please? Thank you.
- Hello (name of person), how are you? (Be sincere but not too serious.)

- My name is _____. Your name has come to me through (where you found it). I am interested in (the subject you are gathering information about) and I am looking for someone who can share some key points or information about the subject. Would you be able to help me?

Listen to the response.
Have your questions ready

2. **Through a referral.**

- Hello, is _____ there please? Thank you.

- Hello _____, how are you? (Be sincere but not too serious.)

- My name is _____ and I was referred to you by (first and last name of that person). I am interested in (the subject you are gathering information about) and I am looking for someone who can share some key points or information about the subject. (First name of the person who provided the referral) has told me that you may be able to assist me with more information.

Listen to the response.
Have your questions ready

LIST OF QUESTIONS TO ASK

NOTE: Some of these questions may not pertain to your subject. Add as many as you can think of and number them in their importance. Ask only three questions per person. Be considerate of people's time.

- Could you tell me about yourself and your experiences in the industry?
- Is your job fulfilling and interesting?
- Are there separate divisions within the organization?
- Does your company/foundation/etc. perform other functions within the industry?
- Do you believe formal training (education) is needed to get into the business?
- Do you know anyone who is in the business who did not take the college/university approach?
- Are there any sites on the Internet that would be helpful or any other materials you could point me to?
- Is there a book or publication you could recommend?
- How is the hiring done in your firm? (grapevine, application, etc.).
- Whom could I contact directly who has the ability to hire new employees?
- Are there any volunteer opportunities within your organization?
- What is the future outlook for this career/cause?
- Is there any literature on your company I could stop by and pick up? (Or have sent to me.)
- Is this company a good one to work for? (Ask this only of an employee, not of an owner.)
- Explain your skills and ask the person what he/she advises you could do.

- Are there two or three people that you would recommend I speak with in regard to this subject? May I use your name?
- Are there special qualifications to get into the industry?
- Are there any exceptions that come to mind?
- Does your company have a website?
- Are there any associations or publications you could recommend?
- May I call you from time to time? Could we possibly meet to discuss this further?
- May I have your full name, title and address?

3.   Thank you very much for your time!

A valuable person to thank is the receptionist. If you ever need to call back . . . Send a thank-you card to each person who offered assistance.

SAMPLE RESPONSES AND QUESTIONS THAT MAY BE ASKED OF YOU

(Your personal statement may come in handy here.)

Q. Why do you want this information?

A. I am very interested in learning about your industry and possibly being employed in it, or volunteering, or _____, and I am gathering information. Your assistance, or that of someone you could suggest, would be greatly appreciated.

Q. *Why are you interested in this particular subject?*

A. It inspires me — motivates me to get up in the morning! I believe the skills that I possess would be well served in this industry.
  • list some of your skills, passions, etc.
  • list some of your experiences.
  • use your "bio" as much as possible.

Q. *What do you plan to be doing five years from now?*

A. Answer honestly and directly about your future goals.

You will get different kinds of questions. Write down all of them so that you're prepared for next time.

SENDING OUT YOUR PACKAGE

These following scripts will guide you through sending your resume or package to the correct person, and how to follow up with that person, afterwards.

"PACKAGE" OR PROPOSAL SIGNIFIES:

- Information you have already gathered and how it relates to the additional information you are seeking.

A PACKAGE MAY INCLUDE:

- A letter on the subject and a summary of your goals; references, letters, and some information about yourself. This is similar to a resume, but includes additional resources.

HOW TO GET THE CORRECT NAME OF THE PERSON TO SEND YOUR PACKAGE/RESUME TO (THIS IS ALSO A GOOD WAY TO OBTAIN INFORMATION ABOUT THE COMPANY):

- Hello (name of person who answered phone and/or, "How are you?"). It is (your name). I am looking to get involved in (your subject) and I have a package I would like to send out to your company. I want to be certain I am sending it to the correct organization. May I ask what your company's specialization is?

    Listen to the response.

Q. Who would be the right person to send my package to? ADDRESS

- Always ask for the full spelling of names and addresses. Simple sounding names can be deceiving, and accuracy is critical.

- You may have additional questions, look at your list of questions and "gathering information" scripts.

If you immediately reach the person on the phone to whom you are sending the package, have some things ready to say from the other scripts. Keep it brief, and try to direct the conversation to sending out your package/resume. Our presentation is often more advanced, clear, and concise on paper, as compared to our phone conversations. Allow your prospective contact to read about you first in order to form a favorable first impression, and then it will be easier for both of you to further build a relationship. At the end of your conversation, remember to thank the person for their kind assistance, and that you appreciate them taking the time out of their busy schedule to speak with you.

(SEND A THANK-YOU CARD)

CALL-BACK SCRIPT

Use this script after you have sent out your package/resume.

IF YOU HAVE THE NAME OF THE PERSON:
- Hello (name of person who answers and/or how are you?). It is (your name) calling. May I please speak to (person to whom I sent letter)? Thank you.
- Hello (name of person). It is (your name) calling. A few days ago I sent you a package/resume in regards to (your project). Did you receive it?
Listen to the response.

Return to your QUESTION SHEET and choose to relate any that you feel would benefit this conversation. Get a meeting if you can. Face to face is always best.

IF YOU DO NOT HAVE THE NAME OF THE PERSON:
- Hello it is (your name) calling, I sent a package/resume a few days ago to your company in regards to (your project). Can you please tell me the name of the person who may have received it?
- May I please speak to him or her? (use their name)
- Hello (name of person). It is (your name) calling. A few days ago I sent you a package/resume in regards to (your project). Did you receive it?

LIsten to their response.

Return to your QUESTIONS TO ASK list.

Get a meeting if you can. Face to face is always best.

SEND A THANK-YOU CARD

COMPARTMENT 5

SHARE THE WEALTH

Knowing where you're going and having support in place is an exciting feeling. But a large part of the journey is always re-evaluating your position. Look at all the new information you have gathered and constantly create conditions to keep that excitement going.

Creating conditions is very personal; find out what works for you. It could be playing some of your favorite music or working out. Some people like their environment to be very quiet and relaxing while others like a lot happening around them. Whatever conditions suit you best, make sure you create them because they have a tremendous influence on your outcome.

Once you are on the road to your dreams and desires, you will realize how more enthused you are about everything you do. Share this wealth with others. Volunteering and sharing your wealth is very important; it can do many things for *you* — and clearly, for others.

Volunteering may not be currently in your plan, but it may be a good idea to include this. A good majority of the people I have studied who are fulfilled and achieved a great deal, volunteer their time and energy in some way. We volunteer to help other people; however, we must also receive something from it ourselves, or we will not continue doing it. We must experience satisfaction for ourselves first, to be able to contribute to others. This might seem a little selfish, but as I have said previously, you must be enthused about the organization and what it stands for to be able to give to others with passion.

Volunteering is an experience that will enhance your life and the lives that you touch.

Mother Teresa, who was probably the most unselfish person this past century, devoted her life to help others. She contributed to help make this a better world. How are *you* going to make the world a better place?

We live in a time where things appear to happen very fast, and this advancement is what we expect. Television presents clips from around the world, from the Olympics, to entertainment, to business deals. We sometimes get frustrated because things are not happening quickly enough for us. Please pace yourself, and give yourself lots of time to accomplish your goals. Everything — everything that will ever have great meaning in your life, will take time. Our lives are not sitcoms on TV that deal with any problem within a 30-minute time frame. You have something very unique and special about you — something that no other person possesses. Take the time to find it, and enjoy the journey *you* design.

What type of life do you want to look back upon?

VOLUNTEER OPPORTUNITIES

SHARE OUR WEALTH (SOW)

In this program, individuals/mentors share their experiences with students in a small classroom setting. The students then ask questions of the mentor. At the end of the presentation (approximately 45 minutes), the facilitator asks the students questions to reflect on.

You can participate in many ways. Call us to find out if there is a program in your area. If there is a program in your area, you can be a mentor, facilitator or coordinator, or recruit mentors for the program. If you do not have a program in your area, we will send you a kit that will help you to start one.

PRIME MENTORS OF CANADA

In this program, an individual/mentor spends one to two hours a week, for an eight- to 12-week period, with one student. The purpose of this program is for the student to learn the process of achievement through the help of a mentor. The mentor does not teach, but rather facilitates learning by directing the students to resources.

To be involved in this program, call us to find out if one has been established in your area. If not, we will send you a kit that will help you to start one.

ENERGIZE YOUR ENTERPRISE (EYE)
A Division of Sanglo Systems Ltd. (Est. 1989)

2325 Hurontario St., Suite 426, Mississauga, Ont. Canada L5A 4K4
(Mailing address only)

Telephone 1-877-778-7709
E-mail: *youth@energizeyourenterprise.com*
Website: www.energizeyourenterprise.com

STEPS TO ACHIEVEMENT AND FULFILLMENT

1. Decide you want to get the most that life has to offer and become fulfilled.
2. Be honest with yourself and follow your heart.
3. Stop justifying why you cannot get to where you want to go.
4. Associate with people who have the same desire as you (associations, clubs, etc.).
5. Find a mentor.
6. Create a Perspective Log.
7. Live as many experiences as you can. Then evaluate those experiences to discover your talents.
8. Don't compete with anyone but yourself.
9. Keep vaccinated against the S&F virus.
10. Get out of, and keep out of, the "societal current." Make your own path.
11. Use your own circumstances to your advantage.
12. Don't let other people's opinions stop you from achieving your desires.
13. Get in motion by doing the 11 exercises.
14. Create a map and enjoy the journey.
15. Share the wealth.

ADDITIONAL TOOLS

www.energizeyourenterprise.com

Click on resource page

MORE TOOLS TO HELP YOU

Below is a list of tools that I believe are exceptional among the many tools that are available. Please go to our website (www.energizeyourenterprise.com) or write down the tools you would like to order and enclose a cheque to our address. And open your toolbox to fulfillment!

Tools for Fulfillment by Greg Dobson	$14.99 paperback
Canadian Achievers and Their Mentors	$22.99 paperback
Uncommon Genius — Denise Shekerjian	$15.99 paperback
Making Time Work for You — Harold L. Taylor	$19.99 paperback

Prices are subject to change. Please consult our website.
Please add 15% sales tax, plus $2.50 for shipping and handling.

ENERGIZE YOUR ENTERPRISE (EYE)
A Division of Sanglo Systems Ltd. (Est. 1989)

2325 Hurontario St., Suite 426, Mississauga, Ont. Canada L5A 4K4
(Mailing address only)

Telephone 1-877-778-7709
E-mail: *youth@energizeyourenterprise.com*
Website:www.energizeyourenterprise.com

Please visit our website for lots of additional tools, resources and web links

THE LAST PAGE

Ahhhhhhh — the last page, a place to start from. Wonder why it is we come here first? I'm sure there is some psychological reason we do this. Maybe it is to see, if at the end, there may be something worthwhile to look back on.

Our lives are like a book. Written day by day. When we get to different chapters, we look back on the various activities in our lives. Some chapters are better than others. Some chapters we would like to rewrite altogether. And some chapters are just plain cool!

What is it that makes some chapters better than others? When you look back, you will see a common denominator in the "cool" chapters. Chances are you were engaged in some sort of regular activity that inspired you. It may have been something very simple or very close to your heart. The key is to turn that one chapter into the whole book!

This book is for the average person, like you and me. It is not for the overachievers who already know what inspires them and have been doing it since they were ten. Although I will say that there are people out there who have accomplished a great deal in financial and material terms, but are still waiting for their *cool* chapter.

The purpose of this book is to give you tools that you can use on a regular basis to be fulfilled. These tools are anything from philosophical to hands-on tools, to get to your destination.

Also, the book is designed to give you information that you can use immediately, not 60 or 100 days from now. We all want our lives to be the best they can be, but sometimes we pick up a self-improvement book that is the size of the Bible and wonder what will get finished first, the book or our life! Some of the contents you may find similar to those motivational-style books, because there are some elements that are universal, regardless of what we choose to accomplish.

The fact of the matter is that many of us do not have the *courage* or the know-how to achieve fulfillment. The tools in the book will help you *cultivate* that courage and trust in yourself to make the choices to get you to your desired destination.

It's time to move forward now — or should I say backward —to the *front* of the book and create your own path, one cool compartment at a time.